Dan, Pop and Bob

Sounds Easy Series

Copyright © Egon Publishers Ltd
and Rosalind Birkett, 1993

ISBN 0 905858 72 7

Designed by Howard Birkett,
Amaryllis Software Ltd, Berkhamsted, Herts

Printed by Streetsprinters, Baldock, Herts

All rights reserved. No part of this book may be reproduced or transmitted in any form or by any means, electronic or mechanical, including photocopying, recording or by any information storage or retrieval system without permission in writing from the publisher.

Published by
Egon Publishers Ltd
Royston Road, Baldock, Herts SG7 6NW

TEACHERS' NOTES

LEVEL 0. PRE-READING BOOKS

These books have been designed to help children with visual sequential memory difficulties. They draw attention to the vowels 'a', 'o', 'i', 'e' and 'u' (in that order). First say the word to the pupil and talk about the picture. The pupil should then trace each letter with a finger, saying the letter sound at the same time and finally say the whole word. Point out the highlighted vowel.

INTRODUCTORY LEVEL AND LEVEL 1. FIRST READING BOOKS

Can be used as a reading scheme, or as supplementary books to Spelling Made Easy, 'Fat Sam' – Introductory Level and 'Sam and the Tramp' – Level 1 (Violet Brand). They gradually introduce new vowel sounds, reinforcing the word families.

Acknowledgements

Special thanks to John and Heather Adkins, the staff and children of Egerton-Rothesay Lower School, Berkhamsted, to Violet Brand for her encouragement and inspiration and of course to my family, Lucy (for Ted), Joanna (for Top the Frog) and my husband Howard, without whom these books would not have been written.

Dan, Pop and Bob

ROSALIND BIRKETT

Introductory Level   Book 3
Sounds Easy Series

EGON PUBLISHERS LTD

Dan the fat man and Pop the cat had a ham in a bag.

Bob the dog ran to the bag.

Dan and Pop stop Bob the dog.

Bob is sad.

Bob ran to his soft mat and sat on it.

Dan, Pop and Bob and the ham.

Dan, Pop and Bob. No ham.